Getting Over
My Parents' Divorce

Written by Maryanne L. Duan, LMFT & Marlene Williams, AMFT
Illustrated by Maryanne L. Duan & Marlene Williams

ISBN 979-8-9876585-2-9

This Book Belongs to

_____

Today's Date: _____|

Draw a Picture of Yourself Here

Introduction

Divorce of parents is a traumatic life event which may contribute to psychological vulnerability in the future. Children experience overwhelming emotions and stress. Exposure to separation of parents is not a traumatic event in itself, but children's potential relational difficulties and their emotional and behavioral problems are more likely to be linked to exposure to the roots of parental conflict. Parental separation and divorce during childhood has been associated with long-term adverse consequences well into adulthood, particularly in adult intimate relationships. Children of divorced parents are at a higher risk of academic difficulties, disorderly behaviors, and depressed mood. However resilient children of divorced parents may be, there exists a feeling of distress over upcoming events where both parents will be present.

Your child's well being is largely determined by the quality of interactions they have with their family members after parental separation. Children's relationship with the noncustodial parent is as significant as the ongoing relationship with the main caretaker. Children benefit from spending a lot of time with each parent, even with parents who have high interpersonal conflict with one another.

Children who close in on themselves and do not express their own suffering may experience withdrawal, introversion, and reduction of emotional expression. Your child may experience various emotions such as anxiety, sadness, guilt, shame, and anger, and she will be better adjusted if she is able to express these emotions and learn coping strategies to overcome the symptoms caused by these emotions.

The authors of this book are practicing marriage and family therapists with 15 years of combined experience working with individuals, couples, children and adolescents, and families. The exercises in this book have been tested to produce positive outcomes with their clients. The exercises help your child examine her own understanding of the situation, process her thoughts and feelings about her parents' divorce, develop a healthier perspective, and make adjustments to this unfortunate event in her life. Your child will learn strategies to work through various emotions and feelings she experiences in this traumatic process. Your child is guided to make her own physical and emotional needs known to the adults who love her so she does not feel uncared for, unimportant, insecure, isolated, or even abandoned.

If your child is under 6 years of age and is not able to fully understand the content in this book, you may read the book to your child, and have your child provide the answers when prompted.

Tools your child will need: a pen, crayons or colored pencils with an eraser.

Are You Ready?

First things first, make sure you have the following items with you every time before you read this book.

- ☐ A pen or pencil
- ☐ Colored Pencils or crayons
- ☐ An Eraser
- ☐ A quiet place with no distraction
- ☐ A toy or something else that makes you feel comforted and calm
- ☐ Your mom or dad nearby if you need help from them

GeT READY

Draw a Picture of Your Family

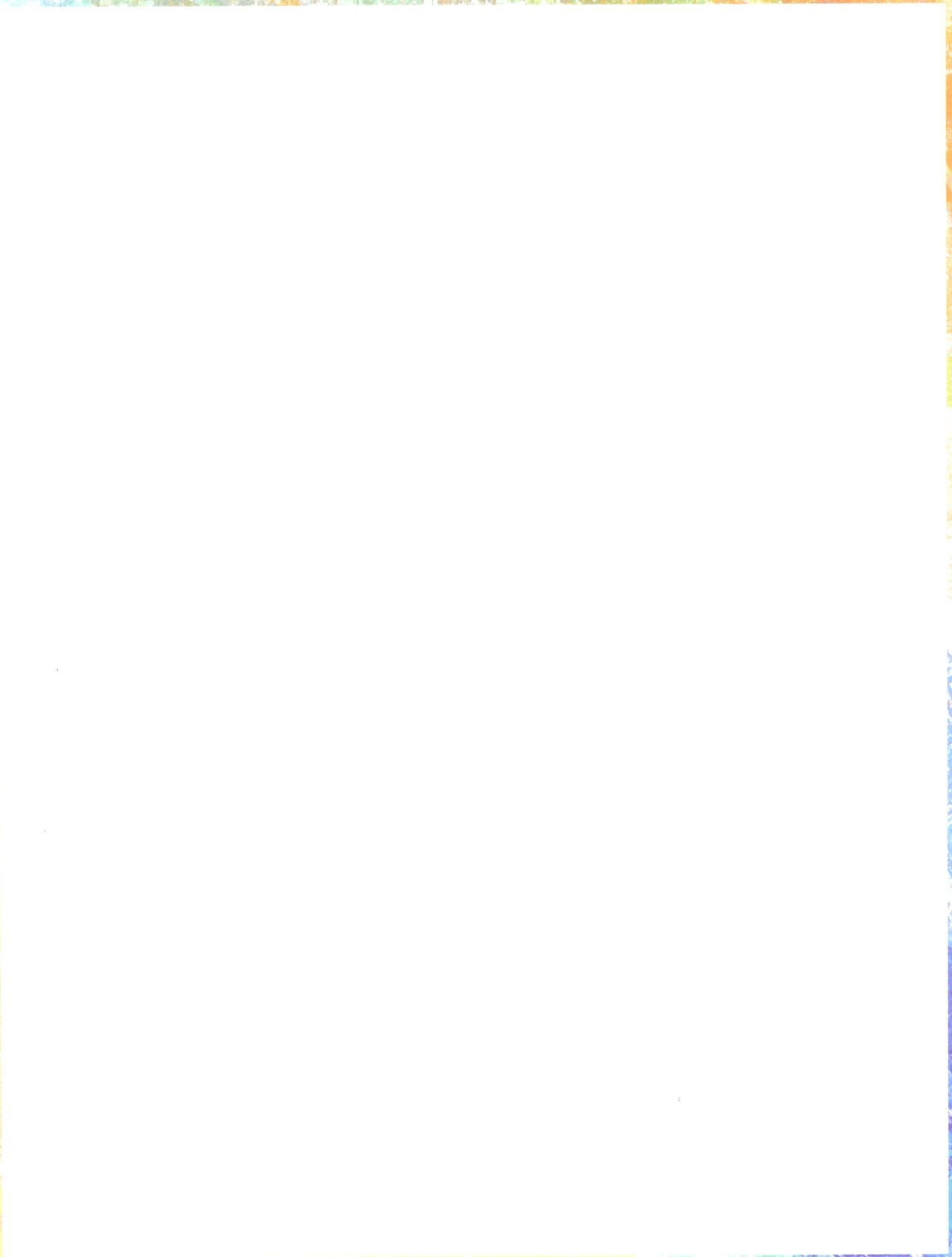

Most of the time, I live with

☐ My Mom ☐ My Dad ☐ My Grandparents ☐ Others

Draw a picture of your room at mom's

What do you like about where you sleep?

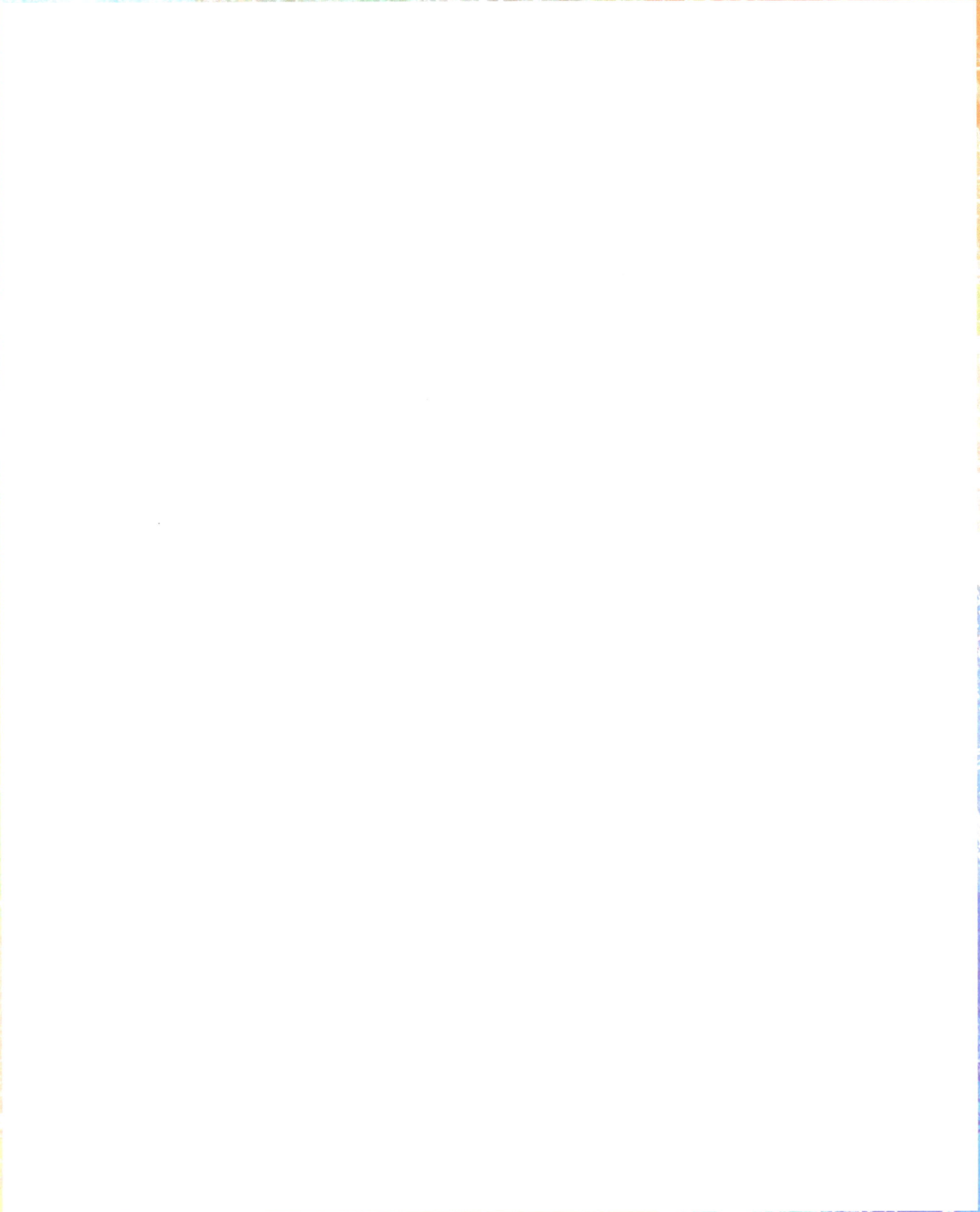

Draw a picture of your room at dad's

What do you like about where you sleep?

Draw a picture of your room at grandparents'

or family members'

What do you like about where you sleep?

Complete the Following Sentences

1. When I feel sad I _____.

2. I like when my parents _____ with me.

3. My favorite game to play with my parents is _____.

4. My favorite memory is _____.

5. I feel frustrated when _____.

6. I talk to _____ when I need help.

7. I feel better when _____.

8. I miss _____.

9. I like to _____before bed.

10. I talk to my mom _____ times per day.

11. I talk to my dad _____ times per day.

12. I worry about _____.

13. I feel scared when _____.

14. I don't like _____.

15. The happiest day was when _____.

16. The worst day was when _____.

17. Other than my parents, _____ also love(s) me.

18. If I could have three wishes, I would wish for:

_____

_____

_____

Draw a Picture of How You are Feeling Now

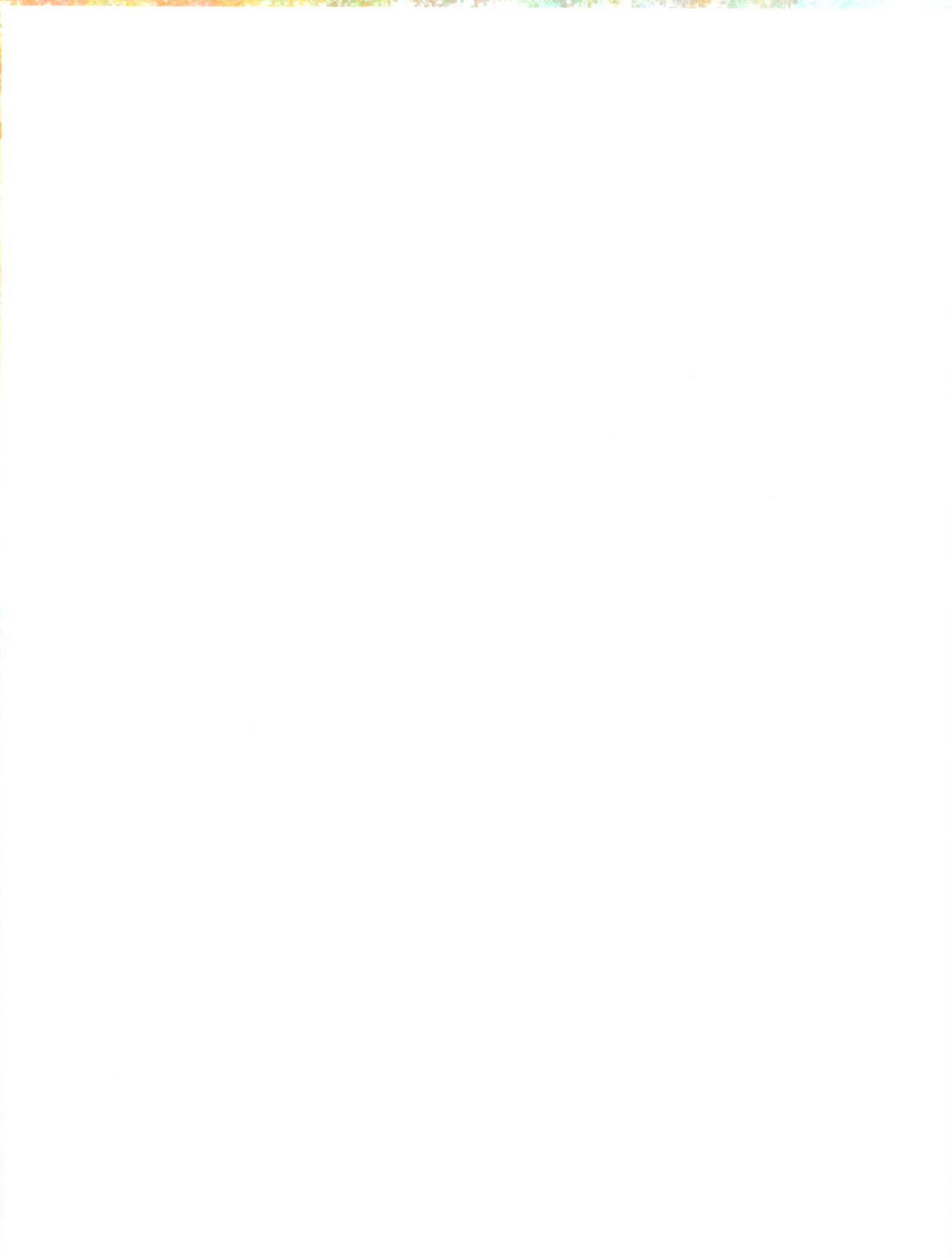

My Parents Are Divorced Because

Check all that apply from the list of possible causes for your parents' divorce:

- ☐ Dislike each other
- ☐ Mom is not keeping the house clean
- ☐ Dad is not helping with the chores
- ☐ They argue about money
- ☐ They are always fighting
- ☐ Dad works all of the time
- ☐ Mom works all of the time
- ☐ Mom is gone all of the time
- ☐ Dad is gone all of the time
- ☐ Mom or dad like someone else
- ☐ One or both of my parents drink a lot
- ☐ One or both of my parents use drugs
- ☐ One of my parents physically hurts the other one
- ☐ Mom and dad do not like to do the same things
- ☐ Mom and dad do not like the other's friends and families
- ☐ Mom and dad do not have the same ideas about how to treat me and my siblings
- ☐ One or both of my parents are mean to the kids
- ☐ One or both of my parents get angry a lot
- ☐ Mom and dad are not talking to each other frequently
- ☐ One of both parents are mean to the dog or cat

IT'S NOT YOUR FAULT!

Sometimes parents get divorced because there are huge differences in their interests, habits, and values. It does not mean that one is better or right and the other is worse or wrong. People are just different.

It's Not Your Fault!

Can you identify some of the differences between your parents?

- ☐ One likes to go out, the other likes to stay home
- ☐ One likes to spend time with family, the other does not
- ☐ One likes to watch tv, the other one likes to play games
- ☐ One likes to eat out, the other likes to cook at home
- ☐ One likes hugs, the other one doesn't
- ☐ One likes a clean house, the other one doesn't care
- ☐ One is always active, the other ones is always on the couch or in bed One likes
- ☐ outdoor activities, the other one does not
- ☐ One likes to try new things and go to new places, the other doesn't One likes
- ☐ to be with friends, the other does not
- ☐ One wants to go to church, the other does not
- ☐ One likes to celebrate birthdays, the other one does not
- ☐ One likes to decorate the house and dress up for holidays, the other does not
- ☐ One is always running late or in a hurry, the other is always on time One goes
- ☐ to bed early, the other goes late

Oh my, people can be so different we are running out of space
and have to go to the next page...

- [ ] One gets up early, the other gets up late
- [ ] One parent or both likes to boss the other one around
- [ ] One or both parents yells at the kid(s) a lot
- [ ] One parent likes to punish the kid(s), the other one does not agree
- [ ] One likes to shower the kid(s) with gifts, the other one doesn't
- [ ] One likes watching sports, the other one does not
- [ ] One likes watching the news, the other one does not
- [ ] They like different presidents
- [ ] They go to different churches
- [ ] One likes to shop a lot, the other one doesn't like it
- [ ] Mom or dad does't want to go to work
- [ ] One is calm and patient, the other one wants things done right away
- [ ] One always looks clean and neat, the other doesn't care how they look and smell
- [ ] One likes to keep the car clean and organized, the other one has a dirty and messy car
- [ ] One or both always forget the other's birthday or anniversary

Can you think of other ways in which your parents are different?:

_____

_____

_____

Can you think of how similar and different you are from your parents?

_____

_____

_____

_____

_____

_____

_____

_____

_____

Why Do Parents Argue and Fight?

Check all that apply from the list of possible causes for the divorce:

- ☐ They do not know how to communicate with each other
- ☐ Whenever they talk, they argue and yell at each other
- ☐ They do not know how to deal with their differences
- ☐ They do not know how to express how they feel
- ☐ They have difficulty telling each other what they want from the other person

- ☐ They are stressed from work but don't know how to get rid of the stress
- ☐ They may suffer from mental illness
- ☐ They may have physical illness or pain
- ☐ They don't know how to meet each other half way

Why Do Parents Argue and Fight?

Can you think of any other reasons why your parents fight and argue?:

_____

_____

_____

_____

_____

Read the Following Sentences Aloud 5 times

My parents are divorced because of their own difference and problems.

It is never my fault that my parents are divorced.

My parents will always love me.

What happens when parents get divorced?

One thing will never change:
Your parents will always love you

Things may be different for you when your parents are divorced

Your parents will always love you

Divorce of your parents means there will be changes in your life. Read through the list and see what are some of the changes you have noticed:

- ☐ They will live in different households.
- ☐ They have different money spending rules
- ☐ They cook different food
- ☐ There are different rules in two houses
- ☐ They arrange furniture differently
- ☐ They celebrate holidays and events differently
- ☐ They bring new friends home a lot
- ☐ They become nicer
- ☐ They become meaner
- ☐ They look happier
- ☐ They look unhappy
- ☐ They are calmer
- ☐ They are more anxious

Wow, there are so many changes than this page can handle, let's go to the next page

- [ ] They are angry more often
- [ ] One or both spend more time with me
- [ ] One or both spend less time with me
- [ ] One or both do not have money most of the time
- [ ] I get more of what I want
- [ ] I get less of what I want
- [ ] I get to do more of what I want to do
- [ ] I get to do less of what I want to do
- [ ] I do more chores
- [ ] I do less chores
- [ ] I go to a new school
- [ ] I have new friends
- [ ] I have no friends
- [ ] I have new clothes
- [ ] I have new toys
- [ ] I spend more time with grandparents
- [ ] I spend more time with others

Can you think of more changes you noticed after your parents got divorced?

_____

_____

_____

Draw a Picture or Write About How Your Parents Look Like or Feel

Do You Know Any One Whose Parents Are Divorced?

_____

_____

_____

What have you noticed or learned about others whose parents are divorced?

_____

_____

_____

The worst things after my parents' divorce have been

_____

_____

_____

_____

_____

_____

Some good things after my parents' divorce have been

_____

_____

_____

_____

_____

_____

Draw a Picture or Write About How You Feel About the Changes in Your Life

How am I feeling?

Your feelings and emotions can change all the time

You may feel differently at times

Complete the following sentence:

I am feeling _____

Other kids have fears about the following things. How about you?

Check everything if you feel the same way

- ☐ They don't love me any more
- ☐ They will leave me some day
- ☐ I will have a new mom or dad
- ☐ I will have to go to a new school
- ☐ I will not see my friends any more
- ☐ One or both parents blame me for the divorce
- ☐ Others thinks it's my fault that my parents are divorced
- ☐ They are not nice to each other
- ☐ One or both parents could hurt the other
- ☐ One or both parents may get sick or die
- ☐ We may not have a place to live in
- ☐ We may not have food
- ☐ We may not have clothes
- ☐ We may not have presents for Christmas or birthdays

Write down your thoughts and emotions
about your parents' divorce
Draw a picture about how you feel

_____

_____

_____

_____

_____

_____

To the Parents

Another aspect responsible for the child's wellbeing is the quality of interactions with family members after separation. Children's relationship with the noncustodial parent is as significant as the ongoing relationship with the main caretaker.

More parenting time spent by the child's father is correlated with a better relationship between child and father. Children benefit from spending a lot of time with each parent, even with parents who have high interpersonal conflict with one another.

Parents are not perfect

- [ ] Some are still learning how to be a parent
- [ ] Some suffer from physical illness that prevent them from being ideal parents.
- [ ] Some suffer from mental illness that prevent them from being ideal parents
- [ ] Some are going through a tough time themselves after divorce
- [ ] Sometimes they may have more responsibilities if they remarry someone else and have more kids
- [ ] Your mom and dad used to take care of you together in the same house, now they are single parent taking care of you alone and may not be able to do it all sometimes

Reaching out to others for love

Make a checkmark next to the people in your life who make you feel loved and cared for (grandparents, uncles, aunts, family friends, god, cousins and siblings, friends, teachers, etc..)

- ☐ grandparents
- ☐ uncles
- ☐ aunts
- ☐ family friends
- ☐ god
- ☐ cousins
- ☐ siblings
- ☐ friends
- ☐ teachers
- ☐ Others: _____

Make a list of people you love

_____

_____

_____

_____

_____

I feel my parents do not love me as much after divorce

Understand your mom or dad is now doing the job of two people. They used to share responsibilities together, but now they are taking on more responsibilities as single parents. They may not be able to do everything and may not be able to spend enough time with you. That does not mean they do not love you anymore.

Your parents will always love you

Your parents will always love you
Parental love for their children
will not change after divorce

I feel loved and cared for when my mom does these things:

_____

_____

_____

_____

_____

I feel loved and cared for when my dad does these things:

_____

_____

_____

_____

_____

Asking Your Parents
When You Need to Feel Loved and Cared for

Make **5** checkmarks next to the things you can ask your parents to do to make you feel loved and attended to. Use the following list for ideas, but feel free to write down anything you would like them to do if it's not on the list:

- ☐ read me a story
- ☐ play with me
- ☐ rub my back
- ☐ going to the ice cream store
- ☐ riding bikes together
- ☐ watch a movie
- ☐ Play a board game together
- ☐ Taking me to the park
- ☐ have cuddle time together
- ☐ Buy me something I like

What are other things you would like your parents to do?

_____

_____

_____

Draw a Picture or Write About What
Your Parents Did to Make Your Feel Better

To the Parents

Anxiety

Anxiety is a feeling of intense distress that can result in worry or fear about an upcoming event. Some anxiety is normal for children to experience, however it becomes a problem when it begins interfering with their daily activities. Divorce or separation of parents can be a stressful event for all in the family, including children. When children experience a flurry of events that they find stressful, they may begin to feel anxious. Such stressful events that occur concurrently with divorce are the moving of homes, the changing of schools, and the addition or separation from other family members. Anxiety can present itself in any of the following ways, but is not limited to: changes in appetite, irritability, frequent worrying, complaining of stomach aches, and difficulty sleeping.

Anxiety

Anxiety is a feeling of fear, uneasiness, and worried thoughts about something.. It might cause you to sweat, feel restless and tense, and your heart may beat faster than usual.

How does it make you feel? Check from the following list and feel free to add your own if they are listed in the list:

- [ ] my heart beats fast or harder
- [ ] my hands are cold
- [ ] my hands are sweaty or wet
- [ ] my stomach hurts
- [ ] I have bad dreams
- [ ] I feel like crying or cry a lot
- [ ] I have headaches
- [ ] I feel like I cannot breathe
- [ ] I feel like hurting myself
- [ ] I cannot focus
- [ ] I feel tired
- [ ] I cannot sit still
- [ ] I feel like something bad is going to happen
- [ ] I have bad dreams or nightmares
- [ ] I feel heavy in my chest
- [ ] I feel nauseated or feel like throwing up
- [ ] I don't feel hungry
- [ ] I feel like my thoughts are racing

OTHER: _____

Which part of your body do you feel anxiety?

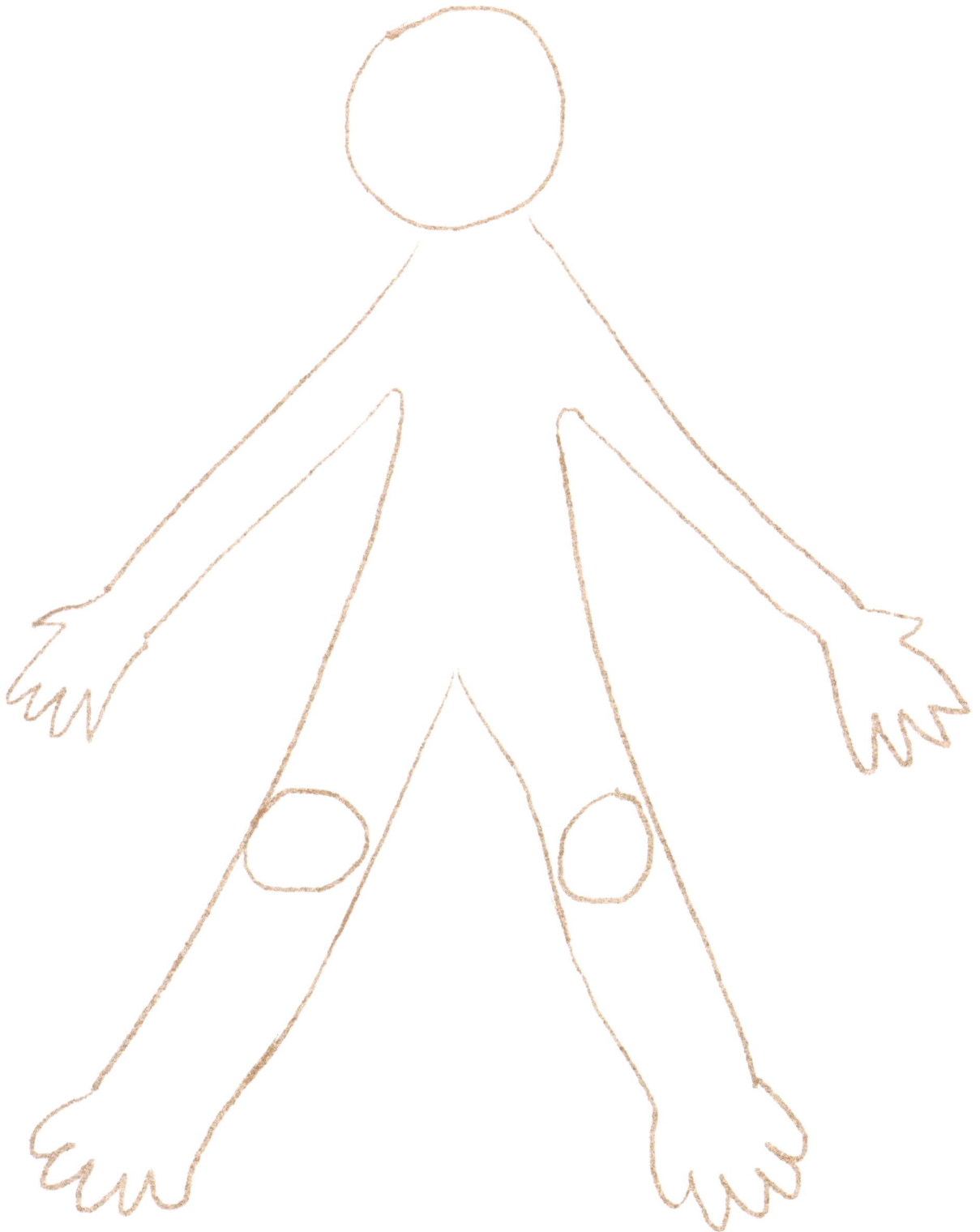

What can you do to feel less anxious?
list of coping skills or strategies

☐ Creating a calming place or area to feel better when you are anxious

☐ Think of a place you like to go and imaging you are there

☐ Gather a few things that make you feel calm and relaxed and hold them when you are feeling anxious

☐ Give yourself a butterfly hug for a few minutes till you feel better

☐ Breath in and out slowly for 10 times. In with your nose, out with your mouth

☐ Make a fist with your hands and count to 5 then release your hands and let go. Repeat two more times.

☐ Listen to your favorite music

☐ Dance to your favorite music

☐ Walking around the block

☐ Riding your bike around the neighborhood like you used to do

☐ Talking to my friends

☐ Talking to my parents

☐ Talking to someone who loves me

☐ Praying to God

☐ Drawing

☐ Playing with a toy or something

☐ Cuddle with your stuffed animal

☐ Petting your pet

What other things can you list here that make you feel better?

_____

_____

_____

_____

_____

_____

What other things can you list here
that make you feel better?

_____

_____

_____

_____

_____

_____

How to create a calming space

Identify a specific room or a spot, or an area in your house you can go to feel better or less anxious. Here are some suggestions, but feel free to come up with your own ideas.

- ☐ My room
- ☐ My bed
- ☐ My closet
- ☐ My bathroom
- ☐ Under a table
- ☐ Under my bed
- ☐ The backyard
- ☐ The living room
- ☐ The kitchen

What other places can you list here that make you feel better?

_____

_____

_____

What are some things you can hold when
you are feeling anxious?
Here are some suggestions, but feel free to add to the list:

- [ ] Stuffed animals
- [ ] My pet
- [ ] A blanket
- [ ] My favorite toy
- [ ] A pillow
- [ ] A squishy ball

_____

_____

_____

How to give yourself a butterfly hug for a few minutes till you feel better?

Remember to breathe and think of the times you felt loved?

It is normal to have doubts, worries and concerns sometimes your parents get divorced. But always remember that your parents will love you even if they are divorced and will do whatever they can to make sure you are taked good care of. You may ask your parents some questions to get rid of some of your worries and concerns.

List of questions to ask parents for assurance

- ☐ Do you still love me as much as you used to?
- ☐ Are you going to leave me?
- ☐ Are we going to live on the streets?
- ☐ Are we going to have no food?
- ☐ Do you think that you are divorced because of me?
- ☐ Am I going to have a stepmom or stepdad?
- ☐ Am I going to have step sisters or step brothers?
- ☐ Am I going to see grandma/grandpa again?
- ☐ Do I still go to the same school?
- ☐ Am I allowed to see my friends again?
- ☐ Are we going to have Christmas as a family?
- ☐ Are we going on vocations as a family?
- ☐ Are you both going to my graduation?
- ☐ Are you both going to my birthday parties?
- ☐ Whose rules am I going to follow?
- ☐ Can we have dinners together sometimes as a family?
- ☐ Are you going to get back together?
- ☐ Am I going to see my uncles/aunts again?
- ☐ Am I going to see my cousins again?

To the Parents

Anger

Anger is amongst the many feelings that children experience in a divorce. Children often display anger through verbal and nonverbal ways, including through play. The inability to manage anger has been correlated with poor functioning in children. Anger is a secondary emotion, which means that there is often another emotion underneath the anger. Children and adults can sometimes have difficulty expressing these other emotions: disappointment, hurt, sadness, worry, guilt, and shame. The anger iceberg can help children uncover which other emotion they may be feeling and identify the reasons for these emotions.

Anger

Do you feel angry sometimes?

Sometimes you may feel angry, but it is important to take a few minutes and try to figure out what you are really feeling inside.

Take a look at the Anger Iceberg picture on the next page. The tip of the iceberg is Anger, that is how you may feel at first. The large portion of the iceberg is usually under the water and can not be seen. Often times, there are emotions and feelings you may be feeling other than Anger.

Anger Iceberg

Can you identify all the other emotions in the lower part of the iceberg?

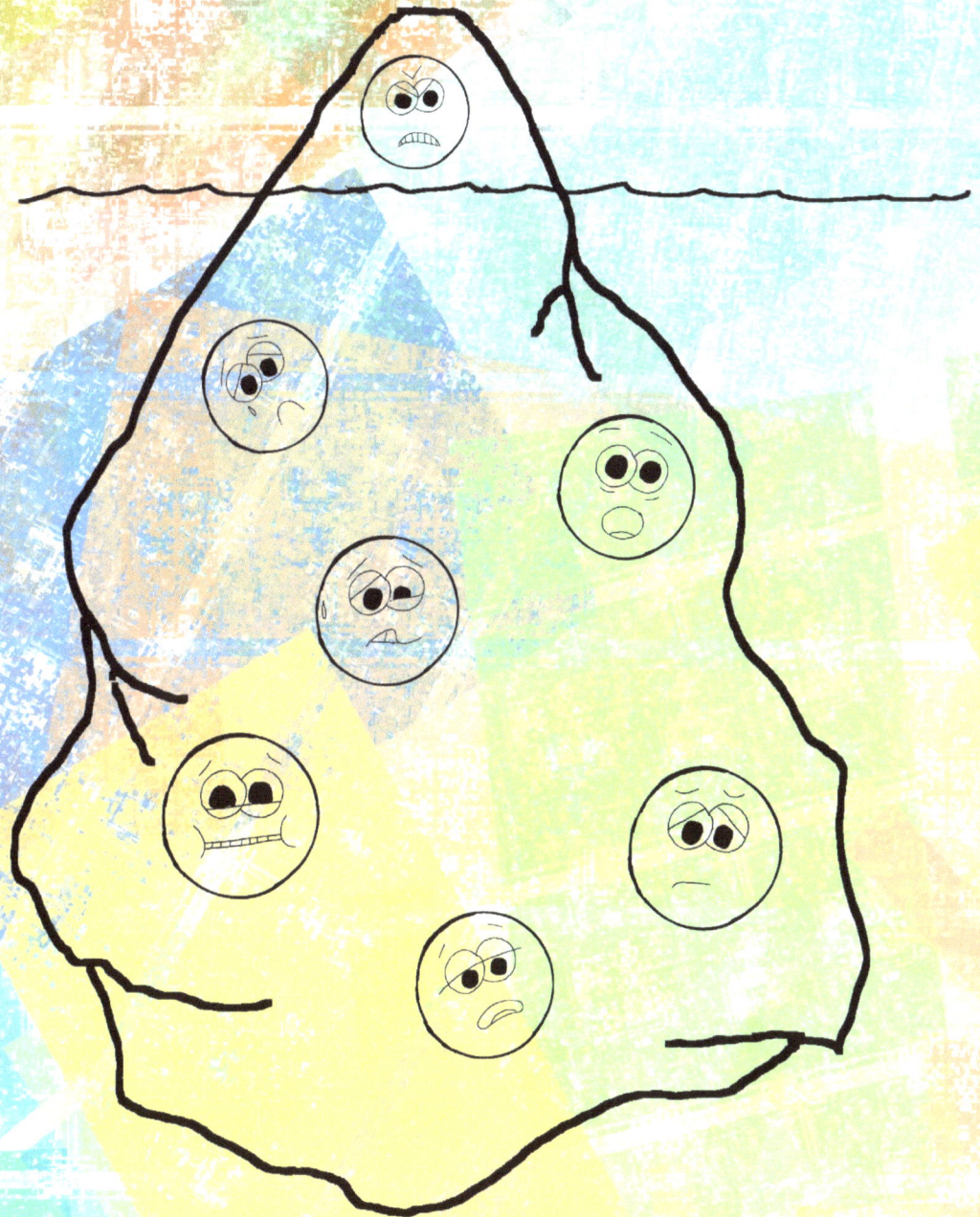

How Do You Know You Are Angry?

- ☐ I feel like breaking something.
- ☐ I feel tight in my stomach
- ☐ I can't breath.
- ☐ My heart beats faster.
- ☐ My legs are getting weak.
- ☐ My arms and legs feel tense.
- ☐ I suddenly need to go to the toilet.
- ☐ My hands are sweating.
- ☐ I have a headache.
- ☐ My face feels hot.
- ☐ I'm breathing faster and heavier.
- ☐ My body starts to shake.
- ☐ I feel lightheaded.
- ☐ My eyes get watery.
- ☐ I feel annoyed.
- ☐ I raise my voice.
- ☐ I try to bother people.
- ☐ I want to hit something.
- ☐ My hands turn into fists.

Complete the Sentences

1. I felt _____ when I was told that my parents were separating.

2. I am angry at _____.

3. I feel angry when my mom says _____.

4. I feel angry when my dad says _____.

5. It makes me angry when _____.

6. When I feel angry, my mom tells me _____.

7. When I feel angry, my dad tells me _____.

8. The last time I felt angry was when _____.

9. When my mom feels angry, she _____.

10. When my dad feels angry, he _____.

11. I express my anger by _____.

12. Sometimes when I feel angry, I also feel _____.

13. Living away from my mom/dad makes me feel _____ and _____.

14. I feel less angry when _____.

How Do You Control Your Anger?

- ☐ Take a deep breath
- ☐ Drink some cold water
- ☐ Count to 100 while taking deep breaths
- ☐ Draw a picture
- ☐ Walk away
- ☐ Do 15 jumping jacks
- ☐ Write down your thoughts or feelings
- ☐ Talk about it with someone
- ☐ Squeeze a stress ball or a tennis ball
- ☐ Play outside till you calm down
- ☐ Listen to your favorite music
- ☐ Read your favorite book
- ☐ Practice a hobby
- ☐ Play with your pet
- ☐ Give your self a butterfly hug

Draw a Picture or Write About the Time When You Controlled Your Anger

Shame

Children of divorce can sometimes experience shame. Shame is a feeling associated with a sense of being flawed as a whole. After divorce, some children feel the need to hide what is occurring in the family from outsiders, despite knowing how common divorce is. When children experience shame, they have created negative judgements of themselves and perceived negative judgements they believe others have made of them. This feeling may come from beliefs that they are unlovable, that they are not enough for their parents to remain together, or that it is somehow their fault that their parents are no longer together. These beliefs can later become internalized.

Shame

Tim, The Little Fox

Tim's mom often bought toys for Tim and his brother. Tim's dad did not like that and would often yell at Tim's mom for buying the toys. One day, Tim's dad asked him "why are you so selfish, asking for toys when you know I don't like it?!" Tim did not know what to say. He felt ashamed at the thought of being seen as selfish. He loved his dad very much and he did not think that receiving toys was a bad thing.

Answer the following questions:

- Why do you think Tim felt shame?
- Do you think Tim did anything wrong? Why or why not?
- Have you ever felt like Tim? Share your story here.

My Story About Feeling Ashamed

To the Parents

Guilt

Guilt is a feeling that people experience when they feel as though they have violated their internal moral standards. Children of divorce can sometimes experience guilt because of their beliefs that they have done something to cause their parents to divorce. Guilt is a common response, especially in younger children, due to their egocentric perspective that others share the same beliefs and feelings as they do. Children may experience guilt, even when told it is not their fault. One of the reasons children may also experience guilt is because they don't have a good understanding about the reasons behind their parents' divorce.

Guilt

Tim, The Little Fox

Tim's dad bought him tickets to his favorite theme park for his birthday, but it looks like there is a problem. Tim's mom already started planning a birthday party for him and sent the invites to most of his friends. Tim now feels like he needs to choose between his parents' gifts. What is he to do? He loves both of his parents very much and does not want to choose one gift over the other. Tim feels guilty at the thought of choosing one. If he chooses his dad's gift, his mom will feel sad. If he chooses the birthday party his mom is throwing for him, his dad will feel sad.

Answer the following questions:

- How is Tim feeling? Write down at least two feelings.
- What should Tim do? Why?
- What can his parents do to help the situation?
- Have you ever had a situation like this? What did you do?

My Story About Feeling Guilty

Living With New Families

What changes have happened in your family since your parents divorced?
Check off the statements that are true for you:

- [ ] My family has separated and lives in two different places.
- [ ] I have a new sister.
- [ ] I have a new brother.
- [ ] I have a stepmom.
- [ ] I have a stepdad.
- [ ] There are more rules that I have to follow.
- [ ] There are less rules that I have to follow.
- [ ] I feel less loved by my parents.
- [ ] The love my parents have for me has not changed.
- [ ] I spend less time with my mom.
- [ ] I spend less time with my dad.
- [ ] My parents fight less.
- [ ] My parents fight more.
- [ ] My parents don't talk at all.
- [ ] We have a new pet.
- [ ] My mom/dad has hired a babysitter to care for me while they work.
- [ ] I spend more time with my grandparents.

Developing New Friendships

- [ ] Saying "Hi" when you meet a new person
- [ ] Feeling comfortable with your new friends
- [ ] Feeling safe around your friends
- [ ] Respect and value your friends opinions and ideas, even when you do not agree
- [ ] Not making fun of your friends or others
- [ ] Laughing at your friends' jokes, but not laughing at them
- [ ] Not calling names or using bad languages
- [ ] Not talking bad about your friends or others behind their backs
- [ ] Respecting your friends' toys and books
- [ ] Sharing your ideas, interests, fun stories, and your toys or books with your friends
- [ ] Playing with or invite your friends to play with you
- [ ] Asking your mom or dad to approach your friends' parents to arrange a playtime
- [ ] Communicating your needs and desires with respect and kindness to your friends
- [ ] Apologizing when you have made a mistake
- [ ] Giving your friends time to express their feelings and desires

My Strengths Checklist

Everyone is different and unique. We all have different strengths and weaknesses. What do you think are your strengths?

- ☐ Wise
- ☐ Empathetic
- ☐ Enthusiastic
- ☐ Fair
- ☐ Modest
- ☐ Grateful
- ☐ Ambitious
- ☐ Athleticism
- ☐ Optimistic
- ☐ Artistic
- ☐ Curious
- ☐ Leader
- ☐ Persistent
- ☐ Social
- ☐ Forgiving
- ☐ Patient
- ☐ Spiritual
- ☐ Smart
- ☐ Generous

- ☐ Logical
- ☐ Adventurous
- ☐ Honest
- ☐ Open Minded
- ☐ Kind
- ☐ Loving
- ☐ Brave
- ☐ Cooperative
- ☐ Common Sense
- ☐ Self-Control
- ☐ Love Learning
- ☐ Funny
- ☐ Creative
- ☐ Confident
- ☐ Disciplined
- ☐ Assertive
- ☐ Independent
- ☐ Flexibile
- ☐ Have self-control

Who Am I?

What Makes ME, ME

I love to play with _____.

I live with _____.

My favorite meal is _____.

I like to listen to this type of music: _____.

I spend most of my time with _____.

I am good at _____.

My biggest strengths are _____.

In the future, I hope that I will be able to _____.

When I grow up, I would like to _____.

What makes me unique is _____.

The happiest day of my life was when _____.

The worst day of my life was when _____.

My favorite toy is _____.

My favorite celebration is _____.

My hero is _____.

These are the things that are most important to me: _____.

These are the people who are most important to me: _____.

My favorite color is _____.

My best friend is _____.

I have fun when I _____.

My family is _____.

I love _____.

I want to be a _____.

I Worry about _____.

Read the Following Sentences Aloud
and Believe They Are True

I am Beautiful

I am Smart

I am Lovable

I am Strong

I am full of love and energy

I can do anything I set my mind to

I am Important and Special

I am grateful for all the good things in my life

I am Proud of myself and my accomplishments

I can do great things

I am in control of my happiness

I can ask help when I need it

I am a blessing to those around me

today, I will be kind to myself

I may fail, but I can get right up again

I like to be challenged so I can grow

Today is a brand new day for me

References

American Academy of Child and Adolescent Psychiatry. (2017, October). Anxiety and Children.

Retrieved from https://www.aacap.org/AACAP/Families_and_Youth/Facts_for_Families/FFF-Guide /The-Anxious-Child-047.aspx The-Anxious-Child-047.aspx

Carmela, M., Desiree, M., Diletta, L. T., Catena, S. M., & Amelia, R. (2019). Family drawing and psychological vulnerability in children's representations of parental divorce. Cogent Psychology, 6(1). https://doi.org/10.1080/23311908.2019.1654723

Ehmke, R. (2022, April 28). Supporting kids during a divorce. Child Mind Institute. Retrieved from https://childmind.org/article/supporting-kids-during-a-divorce/

Ferguson, T. J., Stegge, H., Miller, E. R., & Olsen, M. E. (1999). Guilt, shame, and symptoms in children. Developmental Psychology, 35(2), 347–357. https://doi.org/10.1037/0012-1649.35.2.347

Fidan, B., & Serin, N. B. (2021). An examination of the relationship between anger, aggression, and problem solving skills in secondary school students. Turkish Psychological Counseling and Guidance Journal, 11(63), 577-590. https://doi.org/10.17066/tpdrd.1051426.

Fischer, K. W., Shaver, P. R., & Camochan, P. (1990). How emotions develop and how they organize development. Cognition and Emotion, 4, 81-127. https://doi.org/10.1080/02699939008407142

Motataianu, I. (2015). The relation between anger and emotional synchronization in children from divorced families. Procedia - Social and Behavioral Sciences, 203, 158-162. https://doi.org/10.1016/j.sbspro.2015.08.275.

NHS. (2022, October 18). Anxiety disorders in children. Illnesses & conditions | NHS information Retrieved from October 25, 2022 https://www.nhsinform.scot/illnesses-and-conditions/mental-health/anxiety-disorders-in-children

Wallerstein, J. S., & Kelly, J. B. (1976). The effects of parental divorce: Experiences of the child in later latency. American Journal of Orthopsychiatry, 46(2), 256-269. https://doi.org/10.1111/j.1939-0025.1976.tb00926.x

www.ingramcontent.com/pod-product-compliance
Lightning Source LLC
Chambersburg PA
CBHW042016080426
42735CB00002B/68